Where Is Buffalo Bill?
A Kid's Guide To Cody, Wyoming, USA

Photography By John D. Weigand
Poetry By Penelope Dyan

Bellissima Publishing, LLC
Jamul, California
www.bellissimapublishing.com

copyright © 2012 by Penny D. Weigand and John D. Weigand

All rights reserved. No part of this book may be
reproduced or transmitted in any form or by any means,
electronic or mechanical, including photocopying,
recording, or by any other means, or by any information or
storage retrieval system, without permission from the publisher.

ISBN 978-1-61477-064-0
First Edition

"I could never resist the call of the trail."
BUFFALO BILL

Where is Buffalo Bill?
Bellissima Publishing, LLC

Introduction

William Frederick "Buffalo Bill" Cody (February 26, 1846 - January 10, 1917) was an American soldier, bison hunter and showman. He was born in the Iowa Territory (now the U.S. state of Iowa), in the town of Le Claire. He lived in Canada before moving with his family to the Kansas Territory. Buffalo Bill received the Medal of Honor in 1872 for his service in the US Army as a scout. He was one of the most colorful and inspirational people of the America's Old West; and he became famous for the many wild west shows he organized and in which he performed for over thirty years. He toured Great Britain, Europe and the United States, and in the town of Cody (named after him) he built the famous Irma Hotel, where you can go and stay when you visit the town of Cody on your way to the Yellowstone National Park!

Award winning author, attorney and former teacher Penelope Dyan and photographer John D, Weigand, show you a small part of this grand little town that still captures the unique flavor of the old west as it entertains and delights kids of all ages. If you are a kid, or a kid at heart, this is the place for you! Feel the old west all around you, and let your imagination go wild. Then learn all you can about the old west, and the native Americans who lived off the land and treasured it, and do your best to understand it all and to continue in the preservation of America's treasures.

Rhyme and repetition enhance reading skills as adults encourage young bedding readers to guess what words are coming next in the rhyme. Open a dialog about the old west, and see through the eyes of a child. Learning isn't always about museums and words on a page. What you learn through experience and your own imagination, is what you keep with you forever.

Where is Buffalo Bill?
Bellissima Publishing, LLC

Where Is Buffalo Bill?
A Kid's Guide To Cody, Wyoming, USA

Photography By John D. Weigand
Poetry By Penelope Dyan

Cody, Wyoming, or so I have heard,
is the rodeo capital of the world.
Here cowboys ride broncos
and hope for the prize,
and rodeo princesses dazzle the eyes.
But where is Buffalo Bill?

And if you are there, of course,
you may want to ride a horse!
(But where is Buffalo Bill?)

There are stores filled with things,
like Native American headdresses
and owls with wings.
Of course the owl doesn't fly.
It's just something YOU can buy!
But where is Buffalo Bill?

Here is something original and new.
It's a woman's head carrying a canoe!
But I do NOT see Buffalo Bill!

There's a place in town
where a family can stay,
for an entire week or just for a day.
It is a place that history
knows quite well. . .
It is Buffalo Bill's Irma Hotel!
It was named after his daughter,
in the long, long ago,
and was visited by royalty and others
whose names you might know.
Is Buffalo Bill there?

In an historic room
you can lay your head,
upon a lovely and comfortable bed.
But Buffalo Bill is NOT there!

An antique style radiator
will provide the heat,
so you can warm cold hands and feet!
Has Buffalo Bill been HERE?

You go back down to the restaurant
(you're hungry, after all)
returning down the long, long hall!
You hope it is NOT as you fear,
that the ghosts of things past
remain FOREVER here.
You think about things
that go bump in the night.
Your knees get wobbly. . .
You shake with fright!
Maybe Buffalo Bill is here. . . .

You look back toward your room.
You stop, and then you stare.
Was that the ghost of Buffalo Bill
sitting in that chair?
After all, you know quite well,
Buffalo Bill Cody built this hotel.
Perhaps he NEVER went on his way,
and once you check in. . .
you check in to stay. . . .
Did YOU see Buffalo Bill?

Downstairs in the restaurant
you see the famous cherrywood bar,
a gift to Buffalo Bill
because he was a star.
A gift from Victoria the queen*
who enjoyed a 'Buffalo Bill's Wild
West Show' that she had just seen.
But Buffalo Bill is NOT there!

*At a cost of over $100,000 (to Queen Victoria) in its day, it is worth over a million dollars today.

And just when you think you'll flip,
your parents sign you all up
for a Red River Canyon trip.
And after that. . .
off to Yellowstone National Park
you will drive in your car,
because, after all, it isn't that far!
But you still haven't seen Buffalo Bill!

Then finally you find him,
silhouetted and still!
Right here in Cody is old Buffalo Bill!*

The Scout, a bronze statue of a rider, was placed in 1924 to commemorate the town's most famous resident and de facto founder, Buffalo Bill Cody. It was sculpted by Gertrude Vanderbilt Whitney, and was dedicated to the town of Cody on July 4, 1924.

"...the West of the old times, with its strong characters, its stern battles and its tremendous stretches of loneliness, can never be blotted from my mind."

Buffalo Bill

www.ingramcontent.com/pod-product-compliance
Ingram Content Group UK Ltd.
Pitfield, Milton Keynes, MK11 3LW, UK
UKHW060135240426
12048UKWH00002B/53